2 THREE-COLOR BLANKET
4 TASSEL HAT
6 BUTTONED BOOTIES
7 ICE CREAM CONE RATTLE
10 BABY COCOON
12 CLUSTERS & CROSSES BLANKET
14 VELVET BUNNY
18 RIPPLE WAVES BLANKET
20 EVERYDAY SET
23 SIMPLY SWEET BLANKET
24 CUTIE CUB HAT
26 ROUND BLANKET
28 COZY HOODIE
32 HAPPY BABY BLANKET
34 CLOUDY DAY MOBILE
37 CUFFED BOOTIES
38 QUICK & COZIEST BLANKET
40 SUNSHINE PILLOW
42 BIB & BOOTIES SET

THREE-COLOR BLANKET

Easy

MEASUREMENTS
Approx 43"/109cm x 57"/144.5cm

MATERIALS
Yarn

Bernat® *Baby Sport*™ *Solids*, 12.3oz/350g balls, each approx 1256yd/1148m (acrylic)
- 1 ball in #21128 Baby Blue (A)
- 1 ball in #21230 Baby Green (B)

Bernat® *Softee® Baby*™, 5oz/140g balls, each approx 362yd/331m (acrylic)
- 2 balls #30815 Soft Lilac (C)

Hook
- Size G/6 (4mm) crochet hook, *or size needed to obtain gauge*

GAUGE
16 dc and 9 rows = 4"/10cm using size G/6 (4mm) hook. *TAKE TIME TO CHECK GAUGE.*

NOTES
- Ch 3 at beg of row counts as dc.
- To change color, work to last 2 loops on hook. Draw loop of next color through 2 loops on hook to complete st and proceed in next color.

STRIP I (Make 2)
With A, ch 34.

1st row: (RS) 1 dc in 4th ch from hook. *1 dc in each of next 7 ch. Ch 4. (Yoh) twice. Draw up a loop in next ch. (Yoh and draw through 2 loops on hook) twice. Skip next 5 ch. (Yoh) twice. Draw up a loop in next ch. (Yoh and draw through 2 loops on hook) twice. Yoh and draw through all 3 loops on hook. Ch 4. Rep from * once more. 1 dc in each of last 2 ch. Turn.

**2nd row: Ch 3. 1 dc in next dc. *Ch 7. 1 dc in each of next 7 dc. Rep from * once more. 1 dc in each of last 2 dc. Turn.

3rd row: Ch 3. 1 dc in next dc. *1 dc in each of next 7 dc. Ch 4. 1 sc in top of Tr2tog 2 rows below, working over ch-7 sp. Ch 4. Rep from * once more. 1 dc in each of last 2 dc. Turn.

4th row: Ch 3. 1 dc in next dc. *(1 tr. Ch 5. 1 tr) in next sc—V-st made. 1 dc in each of next 7 dc. Rep from * once more. 1 dc in each of last 2 dc. Turn.

5th row: Ch 3. 1 dc in next dc. *Ch 4. (Yoh) twice. Draw up a loop in next dc. (Yoh and draw through 2 loops on hook) twice. Skip next 5 dc. (Yoh) twice. Draw up a loop in next dc. (Yoh and draw through 2 loops on hook) twice. Yoh and draw through all 3 loops on hook—Tr2tog made. Ch 4. 1 dc in next tr. 5 dc in next ch-5 sp. 1 dc in next tr. Rep from * once more. 1 dc in each of last 2 dc. Turn.

6th row: Ch 3. 1 dc in next dc. *1 dc in each of next 7 dc. Ch 7. Rep from * once more. 1 dc in each of last 2 dc. Turn.

7th row: Ch 3. 1 dc in next dc. *Ch 4. 1 sc in top of Tr2tog 2 rows below, working over ch -7 sp. Ch 4. 1 dc in each of next 7 dc. Rep from * once more. 1 dc in each of last 2 dc. Turn.

8th row: Ch 3. 1 dc in next dc. *1 dc in each of next 7 dc. V-st in next sc. Rep from * once more. 1 dc in each of last 2 dc. Turn.

9th row: Ch 3. 1 dc in next dc. *1 dc in next tr. 5 dc in next ch-5 sp. 1 dc in next tr. Ch 4. Tr2tog over next 7 dc. Ch 4. Rep from * once more. 1 dc in each of last 2 dc. Turn.
Rep 2nd to 4th rows. Break A.
With B, rep 5th to 9th rows, then 2nd to 8th rows. Break B.
** With C, rep 9th, then 2nd to 9th rows, then 2nd to 4th rows. Break C.
With A, rep 5th to 9th rows, then 2nd to 8th rows. Break A.
With B, rep 9th, then 2nd to 9th rows, then 2nd to 4th rows. Break B.
With C, rep 5th to 9th rows, then 2nd to 8th rows. Break C.
Join A. With A, rep 9th row. Rep from ** to ** once more. Fasten off at end of last row.

STRIP II (Make 2)
With B, ch 34.

Work as given for Strip I, substituting B for A, C for B, and A for C.

STRIP III (Make 2)

With C, ch 34. Work as given for Strip I, substituting C for A, A for B, and B for C.

FINISHING

Sew Strips tog in the following sequence: I, II, III, I, II, III.

Edging

1st rnd: Join A with sl st to any corner of Blanket.
Ch 1. Work 1 rnd of sc evenly around Blanket, having 3 sc in corners. Join B with sl st to first sc.

2nd rnd: With B, ch 1. 1 sc in each sc around, having 3 sc in corner sc. Join C with sl st to first sc.

3rd rnd: With C, ch 1. 1 sc in each sc around, having 3 sc in corner sc. Join with sl st to first sc. Fasten off.•

TASSEL HAT

Easy

SIZES
To fit baby head sizes 6–12 (18–24) months

MATERIALS
Yarn (5)
Bernat® *Baby Marly*™, 10.5oz/300g balls, each approx 221yd/202m
• 1 ball in #33004 Buttercream or #33001 Apple Blossom
Note: 1 ball will make 2 Hats.

Hook
• Size L/11 (8mm) crochet hook, *or size needed to obtain gauge*

GAUGE
9 sc and 10 rows = 4"/10cm using size L/11 (8mm) hook.
TAKE TIME TO CHECK GAUGE.

NOTES
• The instructions are written for smaller size. If changes are necessary for larger size the instructions will be written thus ( ).
• Hat is worked sideways.

HAT
Ch 25 (27).
1st row: 1 hdc in 3rd ch from hook. 1 hdc in each ch to last 5 ch. 2 sc in each of next 2 ch. Sl st in each of last 3 ch. Turn.
2nd row: Ch 1. Working in front loops only, sl st in each of first 3 sts. Working in front loops only, 1 sc in

each of next 2 sts. Working in horizontal bar only, created by hdc at front of work (see diagram), 1 hdc in each st to end of row. Turn.

3rd row: Ch 2 (does not count as st). Working in horizontal bar only, created by hdc at front of work, 1 hdc in each st to last 5 sts. Working in front loops only, 1 sc in each of next 2 sc. Working in front loops only, sl st in each of last 3 sts. Turn.

Rep 2nd and 3rd rows until work from beg measures 16 (17)"/40.5 (43)cm. Fasten off, leaving a long end. Weave end through last sl st of each row along top edge and gather tightly. Sew back seam.

FINISHING

Tassel (Make 2)

Cut a piece of cardboard 3"/7.5cm wide. Wind yarn around cardboard 20 times. Break yarn, leaving a long end and thread end through a needle. Slip needle through all loops and tie tightly. Remove cardboard and wind yarn tightly around loops ¾"/1.5cm below fold. Fasten securely. Cut through rem loops and trim ends evenly. Sew Tassel to each side of Hat.•

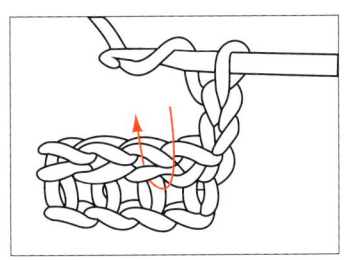

ARROW INDICATES HORIZONTAL BAR TO WORK INTO

BUTTONED BOOTIES

Easy

SIZES
To fit baby foot sizes 3–6 (6–12) months

Yarn
Bernat® *Baby*®, 1¾oz/50g balls, each approx 191yd/175m (acrylic, nylon)
• 1 ball in #35185 Soft Lilac

Hook
• Size D/3 (3.25mm crochet hook, *or size needed to obtain gauge*

Notions
• 2 buttons
• Stitch marker

GAUGE
22 sc and 24 rows = 4"/10cm using size D/3 (3.25mm) hook. *TAKE TIME TO CHECK GAUGE.*

NOTES
• Ch 2 at beg of row does not count as hdc.
• The instructions are written for smaller size. If changes are necessary for larger size the instructions will be written thus ( ).

BOOTIE (Make 2)
Ch 14 (22).
1st row: (RS) 2 sc in 2nd ch from hook. 1 sc in each of next 3 (7) ch. 2 sc in each of next 2 ch. 1 sc in next ch (place marker on last st). 2 sc in each of next 2 ch. 1 sc in each of next 3 (7) ch. 2 sc in last ch. 19 (27) sc. Turn.
2nd row: Ch 1. 2 sc in first sc. 1 sc in each sc to 2 sc before marked sc. 2 sc in each of next 2 sc. 1 sc in marked sc. 2 sc in each of next 2 sc. 1 sc in each sc to last sc. 2 sc in last sc. 25 (33) sts. Turn.
Rep last row 3 times more. 43 (51) sts.
6th row: Ch 2. 1 hdc in each sc to end of row. Turn.
7th row: Ch 2. 1 hdc in first st. *Yoh and draw up a loop around post of next st at front of work inserting hook from right to left. (Yoh and draw through 2 loops on hook) twice—1 dcfp made. 1 hdc in next st. Rep from * to end. Turn.
8th row: Ch 2.1 hdc in first st. *Yoh and draw up a loop around post of next st at back of work inserting hook from right to left. (Yoh and draw through 2 loops on hook) twice—1 dcbp made. 1 hdc in next st. Rep from * to end of row. Turn. Rep last 2 rows once more.
Next row: (RS) Ch 2. (1 sc in next st. Dcfp around next st) 5 (7) times. (Skip next st. Dcfp around next st) 12 times. (1 sc in next st. Dcfp around next st) 4 (6) times. 1 sc in last st. Turn. 31 (39) sts.
Next row: (RS) Ch 1. 1 sc in each of first 9 (13) sts. *[(Yoh and draw up a loop around post of next st at back of work inserting hook from right to left. Yoh and draw through 2 loops on hook) twice. Yoh and draw through all loops on hook – dcbptog made] 3 times.* Dcbp around next st. Rep from * to * once. 1 sc in each of last 9 (13) sts. Fasten off.

STRAP (Make 2)
Ch 33 (40).
1st row: 1 sc in 2nd ch from hook. 1 sc in each ch to end of ch. Turn.
2nd row: Ch 1. 1 sc in first sc. Ch 2. Skip next 2 sc. 1 sc in each sc to end of row. Turn.
3rd row: Ch 1. 1 sc in each sc and 2 sc in ch-2 sp to end of row. Fasten off.

FINISHING
Sew back and sole seam. Sew Strap to Bootie as shown in picture. Sew buttons to correspond to buttonholes.•

ICE CREAM CONE RATTLE

Easy

MEASUREMENTS
Approx 7"/18cm tall

MATERIALS
Yarn

Bernat® Softee® Baby™ Solids, 5oz/140g balls, each approx 362yd/331m (acrylic)
- 1 ball in #30010 Little Mouse (A)
- 1 ball in #02004 Mint or #30205 Prettiest Pink or:

Bernat® Softee® Baby™ Ombres, 4.2oz/120g balls, each 310yd/283m (acrylic)
- 1 ball in #31320 Lavender Lullaby Ombre

Hook
- Size E/4 (3.5mm) crochet hook, *or size needed to obtain gauge*

Notions
- 1 pair of 6mm plastic safety eyes
- Small amount of black embroidery floss for mouth
- Embroidery needle
- Small plastic fillable egg
- Small amount of dried rice or beans
- Stuffing

GAUGE
18 sc and 19 rows = 4"/10cm using size E/4 (3.5mm) crochet hook. *TAKE TIME TO CHECK GAUGE.*

CONE
With A, ch 2.

1st rnd: 4 sc in 2nd ch from hook. Join with sl st to first sc.

2nd rnd: Ch 1. 1 sc in each sc around. Join with sl st to first sc.

3rd rnd: Ch 1. 2 sc in each each sc around. Join with sl st to first sc. 8 sc.

4th and 5th rnds: Ch 1. 1 sc in each sc around. Join with sl st to first sc.

6th rnd: Ch 1. 2 sc in first sc. 1 sc in next sc. *2 sc in next sc. 1 sc in next sc. Rep from * around. Join with sl st to first sc. 12 sc.

7th and 8th rnds: As 4th and 5th rnds.

9th rnd: Ch 1. 2 sc in first sc. 1 sc in next sc. *2 sc in next sc. 1 sc in next sc. Rep from * around. Join with sl st to first sc. 18 sc.

10th and 11th rnds: As 4th and 5th rnds.

ICE CREAM CONE RATTLE

12th rnd: Ch 1. 2 sc in first sc. 1 sc in each of next 2 sc. *2 sc in next sc. 1 sc in each of next 2 sc. Rep from * around. Join with sl st to first sc. 24 sc.

13th and 14th rnds: As 4th and 5th rnds.

15th rnd: Ch 1. 2 sc in first sc. 1 sc in each of next 3 sc. *2 sc in next sc. 1 sc in each of next 3 sc. Rep from * around. Join with sl st to first sc. 30 sc.

16th and 17th rnds: As 4th and 5th rnds.

18th rnd: Ch 1. 2 sc in first sc. 1 sc in each of next 4 sc. *2 sc in next sc. 1 sc in each of next 4 sc. Rep from * around. Join with sl st to first sc. 36 sc.

19th to 26th rnds: Ch 1. 1 sc in each sc around. Join with sl st to first sc. Fasten off at end of last rnd.
Stuff Cone.

SCOOP

With B, ch 2.

1st rnd: 8 sc in 2nd ch from hook. Join with sl st to first sc.

2nd rnd: Ch 1. 2 sc in each sc around. Join with sl st to first sc. 16 sc.

3rd rnd: Ch 1. 1 sc in each sc around. Join with sl st to first sc.

4th rnd: Ch 1. 2 sc in first sc. 1 sc in next sc. *2 sc in next sc. 1 sc in next sc. Rep from * around. Join with sl st to first sc. 24 sc.

5th rnd: As 3rd rnd.

6th rnd: Ch 1. 2 sc in first sc. 1 sc in each of next 2 sc. *2 sc in next sc. 1 sc in each of next 2 sc. Rep from * around. Join with sl st to first sc. 32 sc.

7th rnd: As 3rd rnd.

8th rnd: Ch 1. 2 sc in first sc. 1 sc in each of next 3 sc. *2 sc in next sc. 1 sc in each of next 3 sc. Rep from * around. Join with sl st to first sc. 40 sc.

9th to 16th rnds: Ch 1. 1 sc in each sc around. Join with sl st to first sc.

17th rnd: Ch 1. *1 sc in each of next 8 sc. Sc2tog. Rep from * around. Join with sl st to first sc. 36 sc.

18th rnd: Ch 1. 1 sc in each st around. Join with sl st to first sc. Do not fasten off.

FINISHING

Attach safety eyes as shown in picture. With black embroidery floss, embroider mouth. Fill plastic egg approx halfway with dried rice or beans. Secure egg opening with tape. Stuff Scoop, inserting egg and stuffing around egg.

Join Scoop to Cone

1st rnd: With bottom edge of Scoop and top edge of Cone aligned, ch 1. Working through both thicknesses, work 1 rnd of sc in each sc around, inserting more stuffing as you go. Join with sl st to first sc.

2nd rnd: Skip first sc. *5 dc in next sc. Skip next sc. Sl st in next sc. Skip next sc. Rep from * around. Join with sl st to first dc. Fasten off.•

BABY COCOON

Easy

MEASUREMENTS
Approx 26"/66cm circumference x 21"/53.5cm deep, excluding hood

MATERIALS
Yarn
Bernat® Baby Blanket™, 10½oz/300g balls, each approx 220yd/201m (polyester)
• 2 balls in #04310 Baby Lilac

Hook
• Size K/10½ (6.5mm) crochet hook,
or size needed to obtain gauge

Notions
• 2 stitch markers

GAUGE
9 hdc and 6 rows = 4"/10cm using size K/10½ (6.5mm) hook. *TAKE TIME TO CHECK GAUGE.*

NOTES
• Joining rnd is located at center back of Cocoon.
• Ch 2 at beg of rnds does not count as st.

COCOON
Beg at base, ch 4. Join with sl st to first ch to form ring.
1st rnd: Ch 2. 10 hdc in ring. Join with sl st to first hdc. 10 hdc.
2nd rnd: Ch 2. 2 hdc in each hdc around. Join with sl st to first hdc. 20 hdc.
3rd rnd: Ch 2. 1 hdc in first hdc. 2 hdc in next hdc. *1 hdc in next hdc. 2 hdc in next hdc. Rep from * around. Join with sl st to first hdc. 30 hdc.
4th rnd: Ch 2. 1 hdc in each of first 2 hdc. 2 hdc in next hdc. *1 hdc in each of next 2 hdc. 2 hdc in next hdc. Rep from * around. Join with sl st to first hdc. 40 hdc.
5th rnd: Ch 2. 1 hdc in each of first 3 hdc. 2 hdc in next hdc. *1 hdc in each of next 3 hdc. 2 hdc in next hdc. Rep from * around. Join with sl st to first hdc. 50 hdc.
6th rnd: Ch 2. 1 hdc in each of first 4 hdc. 2 hdc in next hdc. *1 hdc in each of next 4 hdc. 2 hdc in next hdc. Rep from * around. Join with sl st to first hdc. 60 hdc.

Proceed in Texture Pat:
1st rnd: Ch 2. 1 hdc in each st around. Join with sl st to first hdc.
2nd rnd: Ch 2. *1 hdc in next st. (Yoh and draw up a loop. Yoh and draw through 2 loops on hook) 3 times in next stitch. Yoh and draw through all loops on hook—1 bobble made. Rep from * around. Join with sl st to first hdc.
Rep these 2 rnds for Texture Pat until work from beg measures approx 20"/51cm.
Next rnd: Ch 2. 1 hdc in each of first 23 sts. Place marker on last st. 1 hdc in each of next 15 sts. Place marker on last st. 1 hdc in each st to end of rnd. Join with sl st to first hdc. Fasten off.

HOOD
With RS facing, join yarn with sl st in 2nd marked st.
1st row: Ch 2. Work 1 hdc in each st between markers along back edge of work. Turn. 44 hdc.
2nd row: Ch 2. 1 hdc in first st. Hdc2tog. 1 hdc in each of next 38 sts. Hdc2tog. 1 hdc in last st. Turn. 42 hdc.
3rd row: Ch 2. 1 hdc in first st. Hdc2tog. 1 hdc in each of next 36 sts. Hdc2tog. 1 hdc in last st. Turn. 40 hdc.
4th row: Ch 2. 1 hdc in first st. Hdc2tog. 1 hdc in each of next 34 sts. Hdc2tog. 1 hdc in last st. Turn. 38 hdc.
5th row: Ch 2. 1 hdc in first st. Hdc2tog. 1 hdc in each of next 32 sts. Hdc2tog. 1 hdc in last st. Turn. 36 hdc.
6th row: Ch 2. 1 hdc in first st. Hdc2tog. 1 hdc in each of next 30 sts. Hdc2tog. 1 hdc in last st. Turn. 34 hdc.
7th row: Ch 2. 1 hdc in first st. Hdc2tog. 1 hdc in each of next 28 sts. Hdc2tog. 1 hdc in last st. Turn. 32 hdc.
8th to 10th rows: Ch 2. 1 hdc in each st to end of row. Turn.
11th row: Ch 2. 1 hdc in first st. (Hdc2tog) 15 times. 1 hdc in last st. Turn. 17 hdc.
12th row: Ch 2. 1 hdc in each st to end of row. Fasten off.

FINISHING
Fold Hood in half. Sew top Hood seam.•

CLUSTERS & CROSSES BLANKET

Easy

MEASUREMENTS

Approx 36"/91.5cm square

MATERIALS

Yarn

Bernat® Baby Sport™ Solids, 12.3oz/350g balls, each approx 1256yd/1148m (acrylic)
• 1 ball in #21420 Baby Pink or #21128 Baby Blue (A)

Bernat® Baby Sport™ Ombres, 9.8oz/280g balls, each approx 893yd/816m (acrylic)
• 1 ball in #24306 Baby Baby Ombre or #24744 Funny Prints (B)

Hook
• Size G/6 (4mm) crochet hook, or size needed to obtain gauge

GAUGE

7 clusters and 10 rows = 4"/10cm using size G/6 (4mm) hook in pat. *TAKE TIME TO CHECK GAUGE.*

Center Section

With B, ch 98.

1st row: (RS) 1 sc in 2nd ch from hook. 1 sc in each ch to end of row. Turn. 97 sc.

2nd row: Ch 4 (counts as dc and ch 1). Skip next sc. *(Yoh and draw up a loop. Yoh and draw through 2 loops on hook) 3 times in next sc. Yoh and draw through all 4 loops on hook—Cluster made. Ch 1. Skip next sc. Rep from * to last sc. 1 dc in last sc. Turn. 48 Clusters.

3rd row: Ch 1. 1 sc in first dc. *1 sc in next Cluster. 1 sc in next ch-1 sp. Rep from * to last dc. 1 sc in last dc. Turn.
Rep 2nd and 3rd rows 31 times more. Fasten off.

Side Borders

With RS of work facing, join A with sl st to top left corner of Center Section.

**1st row: Ch 1. 1 sc in same sp as sl st. Work 97 sc down left side of Center Section to bottom corner. Turn. 98 sc.

2nd row: Ch 3 (counts as dc). *Skip next sc. 1 dc in each of next 3 sc. 1 dc in skipped sc. Rep from * to last sc. 1 dc in last sc. Turn.

3rd row: Ch 1. 1 sc in each dc across. Turn.
Rep 2nd and 3rd rows 5 times more. Fasten off.** Join A to bottom right corner of Center Section. Rep from ** to ** as given for left side.

Top and Bottom Borders

With RS facing, join A with sl st to top right corner of side border.

***1st row: (RS) Ch 1. 1 sc in same sp as sl st. Work 18 sc along side edge of border. 1 sc in each of next 96 sc across top of blanket. 19 sc across side edge of border. 134 sc.
Rep 2nd and 3rd rows as given for Side Borders 6 times. Fasten off.***
Join A in bottom left corner of side border. Rep from *** to *** as given for Top Border.•

VELVET BUNNY

Intermediate

MEASUREMENTS
Approx 15"/38cm tall

MATERIALS
Yarn
Bernat® *Baby Velvet*®, 10½oz/300g balls, each approx 492yd/450m (polyester)
• 1 ball in #86018 Cuddly Cloud (A)
• 1 ball in #86020 Ever After Pink (B)

Hook
• Size G/6 (4mm) crochet hook, *or size needed to obtain gauge*

Notions
• Polyester fiberfill
• Small amount of black embroidery floss for eyes

GAUGE
16 sc and 17 rows = 4"/10cm using size G/6 (4mm) hook.
TAKE TIME TO CHECK GAUGE.

NOTE
• Join all rnds with sl st to first st.

FIRST LEG
Note: Leg is worked beg at foot.
With B, ch 7.
1st rnd: 1 sc in 2nd ch from hook. 1 sc in each of next 4 ch. 3 sc in last ch. Do not turn. Working in rem loops of foundation ch, 1 sc in each of next 4 ch. 2 sc in last ch. Join. 14 sc.
2nd rnd: Ch 1. 2 sc in first sc. 1 sc in each of next 4 sc. 2 sc in each of next 3 sc. 1 sc in each of next 4 sc. 2 sc in each of next 2 sc. Join. 20 sc.
3rd rnd: Ch 1. 2 sc in first sc. 1 sc in each of next 6 sc. 2 sc in each of next 4 sc. 1 sc in each of next 6 sc. 2 sc in each of next 2 sc. Join. 26 sc.
4th rnd: Ch 1. 1 sc in each sc around. Break B. Join A.
5th rnd: With A, ch 1. Working in back loops only, 1 sc in each sc around. Join.
6th to 8th rnds: Ch 1. Working in both loops, 1 sc in each sc around. Join.
9th rnd: Ch 1. 1 sc in each of next 6 sc. (Sc2tog) 6 times. 1 sc in each of next 8 sc. Join. 20 sts.
10th rnd: Ch 1. 1 sc in each of next 7 sc. (Sc2tog) twice. 1 sc in each of next 9 sc. Join. 18 sts.
11th rnd: Ch 1. 1 sc in each st around. Join. 18 sc.
12th rnd: Ch 1. 1 sc in each sc around. Join.
Rep last rnd until Leg measures approx 5"/12.5cm from 5th rnd. Fasten off.

SECOND LEG
Work as given for First Leg. Do not fasten off. Stuff Legs. Cont as follows for Body:

BODY
Join Legs
1st rnd: With A, ch 1. 1 sc in each of next 7 sc. 1 sc in first sc of First leg. 1 sc in each sc of First leg around. 1 sc in each of rem 12 sc of Second Leg. Join. 36 sc.
2nd rnd: Ch 1. 1 sc in each of next 6 sc. 2 sc in each of next 2 sc. 1 sc in each of next 16 sc. 2 sc in each of next

VELVET BUNNY

2 sc. 1 sc in each sc to end of rnd. Join. 40 sc.

3rd rnd: Ch 1. 1 sc in each sc around. Join.

4th rnd: Ch 1. 1 sc in each of next 27 sc. 2 sc in each of next 2 sc. 1 sc in each sc to end of rnd. Join. 42 sc.

5th to 16th rnds: As 3rd rnd.

17th rnd: Ch 1. 1 sc in each of next 21 sc. (1 sc in next sc. Sc2tog) 7 times. Join. 35 sts.

18th rnd: As 3rd rnd.

19th rnd: Ch 1. (Sc2tog. 1 sc in each of next 5 sc) 3 times. 1 sc in each sc to end of rnd. Join. 32 sts.

20th rnd: As 3rd rnd.

21st rnd: Ch 1. *Sc2tog. 1 sc in each of next 6 sts. Rep from * around. Join. 28 sts.

22nd rnd: As 3rd rnd.

23rd rnd: Ch 1. *Sc2tog. 1 sc in next 2 sc. Rep from * around. Join. 21 sts.

24th rnd: As 3rd rnd.

25th rnd: Ch 1. (Sc2tog. 1 sc in each of next 5 sc) 3 times. Join. 18 sts.

26th rnd: As 3rd rnd. Fasten off.

Stuff Body.

ARMS (Make 2)

With A, ch 2.

1st rnd: 8 sc in 2nd ch from hook. Join. 8 sc.

2nd rnd: Ch 1. 2 sc in each sc in each sc around. Join. 16 sc.

3rd rnd: Ch 1. 2 sc in first sc. 1 sc in each of next 7 sc. 2 sc in next sc. 1 sc in each sc to end of rnd. Join. 18 sc.

4th to 8th rnds: Ch 1. 1 sc in each sc around. Join.

9th rnd: Ch 1. (Sc2tog. 1 sc in each of next 7 sc) twice. Join. 16 sts.

10th to 12th rnds: Ch 1. 1 sc in each st around. Join.

13th rnd: Ch 1. *Sc2tog. 1 sc in each of next 2 sc. Rep from * around. Join. 12 sts.

14th rnd: Ch 1. 1 sc in each st around. Join.

Rep last rnd 10 times more. Fasten off.

Stuff Arms.

HEAD

With A, ch 2.

1st rnd: 8 sc in 2nd ch from hook. Join. 8 sc.

2nd rnd: Ch 1. 2 sc in each sc around. Join. 16 sc.

3rd rnd: Ch 1. *2 sc in next sc. 1 sc in next sc. Rep from * around. Join. 24 sc.

4th rnd: Ch 1. *2 sc in next sc. 1 sc in each of next 2 sc. Rep from * around. Join. 32 sc.

5th rnd: Ch 1. 1 sc in each sc around. Join.

6th rnd: Ch 1. *2 sc in next sc. 1 sc in each of next 3 sc. Rep from * around. Join. 40 sc.

7th rnd: As 5th rnd.

Rep last rnd 7 times more.

Next rnd: Ch 1. *Sc2tog. 1 sc in each of next 3 sc. Rep from * around. Join. 32 sts.

Next rnd: Ch 1. *Sc2tog. 1 sc in each of next 2 sc. Rep from * around. Join. 24 sts.

Next rnd: Ch 1. *Sc2tog. 1 sc in next sc. Rep from * around. Join. 16 sts. Fasten off.

Stuff Head.

OUTER EAR (Make 2)

With A, ch 5.

1st row: 1 sc in 2nd ch from hook. 1 sc in each ch to end of ch. Turn. 4 sc.

2nd row: Ch 1. 2 sc in first sc. 1 sc in each of next 4 sc. 2 sc in last sc. Turn. 6 sc.

3rd and 4th rows: Ch 1. 1 sc in each sc to end of row. Turn.

5th row: Ch 1. 2 sc in first sc. 1 sc in each of next 6 sc. 2 sc in last sc. Turn. 8 sc.

6th and 7th rows: As 3rd and 4th rows.

8th row: Ch 1. 2 sc in first sc. 1 sc in each of next 8 sc. 2 sc in last sc. Turn. 10 sc.

9th to 20th rows: Ch 1. 1 sc in each sc to end of row. Turn.

21st row: Ch 1. Sc2tog. 1 sc in each of next 6 sc. Sc2tog. Turn. 8 sts.

23rd row: Ch 1. Sc2tog. 1 sc in each of next 4 sc. Sc2tog. Turn. 6 sts.

24th row: Ch 1. Sc2tog. 1 sc in each of next 2 sc. Sc2tog. Turn. 4 sts.

25th row: Ch 1. (Sc2tog) twice. Fasten off.

Edging

Join A with sl st to bottom right corner of Ear. Ch 1. Work sc evenly up right side of Ear, having 3 sc in tip of Ear, then down left side. Fasten off.

INNER EAR (Make 2)

With B, work as given for Outer Ear.

Join Ears

With WS of Inner and Outer Ear tog, join A with sl st to bottom right corner of Ear. Working through both thicknesses, work 1 sc in each sc to join Outer and Inner Ear, having 3 sc in center sc at tip of Ear. Fasten off.

FINISHING

Sew Ears to top of Head as shown in picture. With black embroidery floss, embroider eyes using satin stitch. With B, embroider nose and mouth using straight stitch. Attach Head and Arms to Body.•

RIPPLE WAVES BLANKET

Easy

MEASUREMENTS
Approx 30"/76cm x 38"/96.5cm

MATERIALS
Yarn

Bernat® *Baby Coordinates®*, 5oz/140g balls, each approx 388yd/355m (acrylic, rayon, nylon)
- 1 ball in #48128 Soft Blue (A)
- 1 ball in #48005 White (B)
- 1 ball in #48046 Soft Gray (C)

Hook
- Size G/6 (4mm) crochet hook, *or size needed to obtain gauge*

Notion
- Yarn needle

GAUGE
16 sc and 19 rows = 4"/10cm with size G/6 (4mm) hook.
TAKE TIME TO CHECK GAUGE.

BLANKET
With A, ch 163.

1st row: (RS) 3 dc in 4th ch from hook. (Skip next 2 ch. 3 dc in next ch) twice. Skip next 2 ch. (3 dc. Ch 3. 3 dc) in next ch. *(Skip next 2 ch. 3 dc in next ch) twice. Skip next 2 ch. (Yoh and draw up a loop. Yoh and draw through 2 loops on hook) 3 times in next ch. Yoh and draw through all 4 loops on hook—CL made. Skip next 4 ch. CL in next ch. (Skip next 2 ch. 3 dc in next ch) twice. Skip next 2 ch. (3 dc. Ch 3. 3 dc) in next ch. Rep from * to last 12 ch. Skip next 2 ch. (3 dc in next ch. Skip next 2 ch) 3 times. 1 dc in last ch. Turn.

Note: Work sts of following rows in sps between groups of 3 dc or CL.

2nd row: Ch 3 (counts as dc). Skip first sp (between turning ch and next group of 3 dc). 3 dc in each of next 3 sps. (3 dc. Ch 3. 3 dc) in next ch-3 sp. *(3 dc in next sp) twice. CL in next sp. Skip next sp (between CL). CL in next sp. (3 dc in next sp) twice. (3 dc. Ch 3. 3 dc) in next ch-3 sp. Rep from * to last 4 sps. (3 dc in next sp) 3 times. 1 dc in last sp (between last group of 3 dc and turning ch). Join B. Turn.

Last row forms pat.

Cont in pat and proceed in Stripe Pat as follows:
(1 row B, 2 rows C) twice, (1 row B, 2 rows A) twice. These 12 rows form Stripe Pat.

Work a further 45 rows in Stripe Pat (59 rows total have been worked), ending on 2 rows of A. Fasten off.

FINISHING
Side Edging
With RS facing, join A with sl st at top corner of Blanket. Ch 1. Work 1 row of sc evenly down side edge. Fasten off.
Rep across opposite side edge.•

EVERYDAY SET

Easy

SIZES
To fit size 6–12 mos.

MATERIALS
Yarn
Bernat® *Handicrafter*® *Cotton*, 1¾oz/50g balls, each approx 80yd/73m (cotton)
- 2 balls in color of your choice (A)
- 1 ball in #01001 White (B)

Hook
- Size G/6 (4mm) crochet hook, *or size needed to obtain gauge*

Notions
- Button
- Yarn needle

GAUGE
14 sc and 16 rows = 4"/10cm using size G/6 (4mm) hook. *TAKE TIME TO CHECK GAUGE.*

BIB
With A, ch 20
1st row: (RS) 1 sc in 2nd ch from hook. 1 sc in each ch to end of ch. Turn. 19 sts.
2nd row: Ch 1. 2 sc in first st. 1 sc in each st to last st. 2 sc in last st. Ch 1. Turn.
3rd row: 1 sc in each st to end of row. Turn.
4th to 9th rows: Rep last 2 rows 3 times more. 27 sts. Cont even until work from beg measures 6½"/16.5cm, ending with RS facing for next row.

Shape Neck
1st row: (RS) Ch 1. 1 sc in each of first 6 sts. Yoh and draw up a loop in each of next 2 sts. Yoh and draw through all 3 loops on hook – sc2tog made. Turn. Leave rem sts unworked.
2nd row: Ch 1. Sc2tog over first 2 sts. 1 sc in each st to end of row. Turn.
3rd row: Ch 1. 1 sc in each st to last 2 sts. Sc2tog over last 2 sts. Turn. 5 sts. Work 10 rows even.
Next row: (WS) Ch 1. 2 sc in first st. 1 sc in each st to last 2 sts. Sc2tog. Turn.
Next row: Ch 1. Sc2tog. 1 sc in each st to last st. 2 sc in last st. Turn. Rep last 2 rows twice more. Fasten off. With RS of work facing, skip next 11 sts. Join A with sl st to next st. Ch 1. Sc2tog over this st and next st. 1 sc in each st to end of row. Turn. Work to correspond to first side, reversing all shapings.

Edging
Join B with sl st to top left corner of neck edge. Ch 1. 1 sc in same sp as last sl st. Work 1 row sc evenly around all edges. Join with sl st to first sc.
Next rnd: Working around outer edge only, ch 1. *1 sc in each of next 3 sts. Ch 3. Ss in first ch—picot made. Rep from * to opposite side. Fasten off. With B, make button loop at center back on left side. Sew button in position. If desired, embroider day of week onto bib as illustrated. With B, split yarn into 2 plies and embroider letters using chain stitch.

BOOTIE (Make 2)
With A, ch 16.
1st row: (RS) 1 sc in 2nd ch from hook. 1 sc in each ch to end of ch. Turn. 15 sts.
2nd row: Working into back loop only of each st, ch 1. Work 1 sc in each st to end of row. Turn. Rep last row until work from beg measures 6¼"/16cm when slightly stretched. Do not fasten off.
1st row: (RS) Ch 1. Work 23 sc evenly across long edge of cuff. Join B. Turn.
2nd row: With B, ch 1. Work 1 sc in each sc to end of row. Fasten off.

Instep

1st row: With RS of work facing, skip first 7 sts. Join B with sl st to next st. Ch 1. 1 sc in same sp. 1 sc in each of next 8 sts. Turn. 9 sts.

2nd to 4th rows: Ch 1. 1 sc in each st to end of row. Turn.

5th row: Ch 1. Sc2tog. 1 sc in each of next 5 sts. Sc2tog. Turn.

6th row: Ch 1. Sc2tog. 1 sc in each of next 3 sts. Sc2tog. Fasten off. Sew center back seam. With RS of work facing, join B with sl st at center back. Ch 1. 1 sc in each of next 7 sts. Work 5 sc down side of instep. 3 sc in corner sc. 3 sc across end of instep. 3 sc in corner sc. Work 5 sc along other side of instep. 1 sc in each of next 7 sts. Join with sl st to first st. 33 sts.

EVERYDAY SET

Next rnd: Ch 1. 1 sc in each st around. Join with sl st to first st.

Next rnd: Ch 1. 1 sc in each st around. Join A with sl st to first st.

Next rnd: With A, ch 1. Working in back loops only, work 1 sc in each st around. Join with sl st to first st.

Next rnd: Ch 1. Sc2tog. 1 sc in each of next 12 sts. Sc2tog. 1 sc in next st. Sc2tog. 1 sc in each of next 12 sts. Sc2tog. Join with sl st to first st.

Next rnd: Ch 1. Sc2tog. 1 sc in each of next 10 sts. Sc2tog. 1 sc in next st. Sc2tog. 1 sc in each of next 10 sts. Sc2tog. Join with sl st to first st.

Next rnd: Ch 1. Sc2tog. 1 sc in each of next 8 sts. Sc2tog. 1 sc in next st. Sc2tog. 1 sc in each of next 8 sts. Sc2tog. Join with sl st to first st. Fasten off. Join center foot seam.

FINISHING

Using the words below as a guide, chain stitch the day of the week to the bib. •

CHAIN STITCH

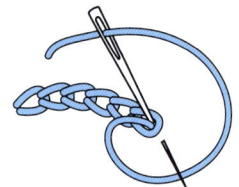

sunday
monday
tuesday
wednesday
thursday
friday
saturday

SIMPLY SWEET BLANKET

Easy

MEASUREMENTS
Approx 36"/91.5cm wide x 38"/96.5cm long

MATERIALS
Yarn
Bernat® *Baby Sport*™, 12.3oz/350g balls, each 1256yd/1148m (acrylic)
• 2 balls in #21230 Baby Green

Hook
• Size G/6 (4mm) crochet hook, *or size needed to obtain gauge*

GAUGE
19 dc and 10 rows = 4"/10cm using size G/6 (4mm) hook. *TAKE TIME TO CHECK GAUGE*

NOTE
• Ch 3 at beg of row counts as 1 dc.

BLANKET
Ch 162.
Foundation row: (RS) 1 dc in 3rd ch from hook (counts as 2 dc). *Ch 1. Skip next 2 ch. 3 dc in next ch. Rep from * to last 3 ch. Ch 1. Skip next 2 ch. 2 dc in last ch. Turn. 52 3-dc groups.
1st row: Ch 3. Skip first 2 dc. *(1 dc. Ch 1. 1 dc) in next ch-1 sp – V-st made. Rep from * to last 2 dc. Skip next dc. 1 dc in top of turning ch. Turn. 53 V-sts.
2nd row: Ch 3. *3 dc in ch-1 sp of next V-st. Ch 1. Rep from * to last V-st. 3 dc in last V-st. 1 dc in top of turning ch. Turn.
3rd row: Ch 3. 1 dc in first dc. *1 V-st in next ch-1 sp. Rep from * to last dc. 2 dc in top of turning ch. Turn.
4th row: Ch 3. 1 dc in next dc. Ch 1. *3 dc in ch-1 sp of next V-st. Ch 1. Rep from * to last 2 dc. 1 dc in next dc. 1 dc in top of turning ch. Turn. Rep last 4 rows until work from beg measures 35"/89cm, ending with 4th row of pat. Do not fasten off.

FINISHING
Edging
1st rnd: Ch 1. Work 1 rnd of sc evenly around Blanket, having 3 sc in corners. Join with sl st to first sc.
2nd rnd: Ch 1. 1 sc in first sc. *Ch 3. Sl st in top of sc—picot made. 1 sc in each of next 2 sc. Rep from * around. Join with sl st to first sc. Fasten off.•

CUTIE CUB HAT

Easy

SIZES
To fit baby head sizes 6–12 (18–24) months.

MATERIALS
Yarn
Bernat® *Baby Velvet*™, 10½oz/300g balls, each approx 492yd/450m (polyester)
• 1 ball in #86028 Bunny Brown

Hook
• Size G/6 (4mm) crochet hook, *or size needed to obtain gauge*

Notion
• Tapestry needle

GAUGE
15 hdc and 14 rows = 4"/10cm with size G/6 (4mm) hook.
TAKE TIME TO CHECK GAUGE.

NOTES
• Ch 2 at beg of rnd does not count as hdc.
• Hat is worked from top down.

HAT
Ch 3.
1st rnd: 8 hdc in 3rd ch from hook.
2nd rnd: Ch 2. 2 hdc in each hdc around. Join with sl st to top of ch 2. 16 hdc.
3rd rnd: Ch 2. 2 hdc in first hdc. *1 hdc in next hdc. 2 hdc in next hdc. Rep from * to last hdc. 1 hdc in last hdc. Join with sl st to top of ch 2. 24 hdc.
4th rnd: Ch 2. 2 hdc in first hdc. *1 hdc in each of next 2 hdc. 2 hdc in next hdc. Rep from * to last 2 hdc. 1 hdc in each of last 2 hdc. Join with sl st to top of ch 2. 32 hdc.
5th rnd: Ch 2. 2 hdc in first hdc. *1 hdc in each of next 3 hdc. 2 hdc in next hdc. Rep from * to last 3 hdc. 1 hdc in each of last 3 hdc. Join with sl st to top of ch 2. 40 hdc.
6th rnd: Ch 2. 2 hdc in first hdc. *1 hdc in each of next 4 hdc. 2 hdc in next hdc. Rep from * to last 4 hdc. 1 hdc in each of last 4 hdc. Join with sl st to top of ch 2. 48 hdc.
7th rnd: Ch 2. 1 hdc in each hdc around. Join with sl st to top of ch 2.

Size 18–24 mos only
8th rnd: Ch 2. 2 hdc in first hdc. *1 hdc in each of next 5 hdc. 2 hdc in next hdc. Rep from * to last 5 hdc. 1 hdc in each of last 5 hdc. Join with sl st to top of ch 2. 56 hdc.

All sizes
Next rnd: As 7th rnd.
Next rnd: Ch 2. 2 hdc in first hdc. 1 hdc in each of next 11 (13) hdc. *2 hdc in next hdc. 1 hdc in each of next 11 (13) hdc. Rep from * around. Join with sl st to top of ch 2. 52 (60) hdc.
Next rnd: Ch 2. 1 hdc in each hdc around. Join with sl st to top of ch 2.
Rep last rnd until Hat from top measures approx 5½ (6½)"/14 (16.5)cm.

Ribbing
1st rnd: Ch 2. *Dcfp around next st. Dcbp around next st. Rep from * around. Join with sl st to top of ch 2. Rep last rnd twice more. Fasten off at end of last rnd.

EARS (Make 2)
Ch 2.
1st rnd: 8 sc in 2nd ch from hook. Join with sl st to first sc.
2nd rnd: Ch 1. 2 sc in each sc around. Join with sl st to first sc.
Rep last rnd 4 times more. Fasten off at end of last rnd, leaving a long end for sewing Ear to Hat.

FINISHING
Sew Ears to top of Hat as shown in picture.•

25

ROUND BLANKET

Easy

MEASUREMENTS
Approx 42"/106.5cm in diameter

MATERIALS
Yarn
Bernat® *Baby Sport*™ *Ombres*, 9.8oz/280g balls, each approx 893yd/816m (acrylic)
• 2 balls in #24306 Baby Baby Ombre

Hook
• Size H/8 (5mm) crochet hook, *or size needed to obtain gauge*

GAUGE
15 dc and 8½ rows = 4"/10cm using size H/8 (5mm) hook. *TAKE TIME TO CHECK GAUGE.*

BLANKET
Ch 4. Join in ring.

1st rnd: Ch 2 (does not count as st). 8 hdc in ring. Join with sl st to first hdc. 8 hdc.

2nd rnd: Ch 3 (counts as dc). 1 dc in same sp as sl st. 2 dc in each hdc around. Join with sl st to first hdc. 16 dc.

3rd rnd: Ch 3 (counts as dc). 1 dc in same sp as sl st. 2 dc in each dc around. Join with sl st to first dc. 32 dc.

4th rnd: Ch 3. (Yoh and draw up a loop in same sp as sl st. Yoh and draw through 2 loops on hook) twice. Yoh and draw through all 3 loops on hook—Beg Cluster made. *Ch 2. Skip next dc. (Yoh and draw up a loop. Yoh and draw through 2 loops on hook) 3 times in next dc. Yoh and draw through all 4 loops on hook—Cluster made. Rep from * around. Ch 2. Skip last dc. Join with sl st to Beg Cluster.

5th rnd: Sl st in next ch-2 sp. (Beg Cluster. Ch 2. Cluster) in same sp as sl st. *Ch 2. Cluster in next ch-2 sp. Ch 2. (Cluster. Ch 2. Cluster) in next ch-2 sp. Rep from * around, ending with Ch 2. Cluster in next ch-2 sp. Ch 2. Join with sl st to Beg Cluster.

6th rnd: Sl st in next ch-2 sp. (Beg Cluster. Ch 2. Cluster) in same sp as sl st. *(Ch 2. Cluster in next ch-2 sp) twice. Ch 2. (Cluster. Ch 2. Cluster) in next ch-2 sp. Rep from * around, ending with (Ch 2. Cluster in next ch-2 sp) twice. Ch 2. Join with sl st to Beg Cluster.

7th rnd: Sl st in next ch-2 sp. (Beg Cluster. Ch 2. Cluster) in same sp as sl st. *(Ch 2. Cluster in next ch-2 sp) 3 times. Ch 2. (Cluster. Ch 2. Cluster) in next ch-2 sp. Rep from * around, ending with (Ch 2. Cluster in next ch-2 sp) 3 times. Ch 2. Join with sl st to Beg Cluster.

8th rnd: Sl st in next ch-2 sp. (Beg Cluster. Ch 2. Cluster) in same sp as sl st. *(Ch 2. Cluster in next ch-2 sp) 4 times. Ch 2. (Cluster. Ch 2. Cluster) in next ch-2 sp. Rep from * around, ending with (Ch 2. Cluster in next ch-2 sp) 4 times. Ch 2. Join with sl st to Beg Cluster.

9th rnd: Sl st in next ch-2 sp. (Beg Cluster. Ch 2. Cluster) in same sp as sl st. *(Ch 2. Cluster in next ch-2 sp) 5 times. Ch 2. (Cluster. Ch 2. Cluster) in next ch-2 sp. Rep from * around, ending with (Ch 2. Cluster in next ch-2 sp) 5 times. Ch 2. Join with sl st to Beg Cluster.

Cont in same manner, having 1 more Cluster between corners on every rnd until:

"Next rnd: Sl st in next ch-2 sp. (Beg Cluster. Ch 2. Cluster) in same sp as sl st. *(Ch 2. Cluster in next ch-2 sp) 29 times. Ch 2. (Cluster. Ch 2. Cluster) in next ch-2 sp. Rep from * around, ending with (Ch 2. Cluster in next ch-2 sp) 29 times. Ch 2. Join with sl st to Beg Cluster" has been worked.

FINISHING

1st rnd: Ch 5 (counts as tr and ch 1). [(1 tr. Ch 1) 5 times. 1 tr] in same sp as sl st. *Skip next Cluster. **1 sc in next Cluster. [(1 tr. Ch 1) 4 times. 1 tr] in next Cluster. Rep from ** 12 times more. Skip next Cluster. 1 sc in next Cluster. [(1 tr. Ch 1) 7 times. 1 tr] in next corner ch-2 sp. Rep from * around, ending with: Skip next Cluster. **1 sc in next Cluster. [(1 tr. Ch 1) 4 times. 1 tr] in next Cluster. Rep from ** 12 times more. Skip next Cluster. 1 sc in next Cluster. Join with sl st to 4th ch of ch 5.

2nd rnd: Ch 1. 1 sc in first ch-1 sp. *(Ch 3. 1 sc in next ch-1 sp) 5 times. Ch 3. Sl st in next sc. [(Ch 3. 1 sc in next ch-1 sp) 4 times. Ch 3. Sl st in next sc] 12 times. Rep from * around, ending with: [(Ch 3. 1 sc in next ch-1 sp) 4 times. Ch 3. Sl st in next sc] 12 times. Ch 3. Join with sl st to first sc. Fasten off.•

COZY HOODIE

Easy

SIZES

To Fit Chest Measurement
6 mos: 17"/43cm
12 mos: 18"/45.5cm
18 mos: 19"/48.5cm
24 mos: 20"/51cm

Finished Chest
6 mos: 20"/51cm
12 mos: 21"/53cm
18 mos: 22"/56cm
24 mos: 23"/58.5cm

MATERIALS

Yarn
Bernat® Softee® Baby™, 5oz/140g balls, each approx 362yd/331m (acrylic)
• 2 (2-3-3) balls in #30044 Flannel

Hook
• Size G/6 (4mm) crochet hook, *or size needed to obtain gauge*

Notions
• Stitch markers
• 4 buttons

GAUGE

16 sts and 12 rows = 4"/10cm using size G/6 (4mm) hook in pat. *TAKE TIME TO CHECK GAUGE.*

NOTE

• The instructions are written for smallest size. If changes are necessary for larger sizes the instructions will be written thus ( ).

BACK

Ch 42 (44-46-48).
1st row: (RS) 1 sc in 2nd ch from hook. *1 dc in next ch. 1 sc in next ch. Rep from * to end of chain. Turn. 41 (43-45-47) sts.
2nd row: Ch 3 (counts as dc). *1 sc in next dc. 1 dc in next sc. Rep from * to end of row. Turn.
3rd row: Ch 1. 1 sc in first dc. *1 dc in next sc. 1 sc in next dc. Rep from * to end of row. Turn.
Rep last 2 rows for pat until work from beg measures 7 (7½-8-8½)"/18 (19-20.5-21.5)cm, ending on a WS row.

Shape Armholes
Next row: (RS) Sl st across first 3 sts. Ch 1. 1 sc in same sp as last sl st. Cont in pat to last 2 sts. Turn. Leave rem 2 sts unworked.
Cont even in pat over rem 37 (39-41-43) sts until armhole measures 4 (4½-4½-5)"/10 (11.5-11.5-12.5)cm, ending on a WS row. Fasten off.

RIGHT FRONT

**Ch 32 (34-36-38).
1st row: (RS) 1 sc in 2nd ch from hook. *1 dc in next ch. 1 sc in next ch. Rep from * to end of chain. Turn. 31 (33-35-37) sts.
Cont in pat as given for Back until work from beg measures 7 (7½-8-8½)"/18 (19-20.5-21.5)cm, ending on a WS row.**

Shape Armhole
Next row: (RS) Work in pat to last 2 sts. Turn. Leave rem sts unworked.
Cont even in pat over rem 29 (31-33-35) sts until armhole measures 6 rows less than Back, ending on a WS row. Fasten off.

Shape Neck
1st row: (RS) Skip first 13 (14-16-17) sts. Join yarn with sl st to next st. Ch 2 (does not count as st). Hdc2tog over same st as last sl st and next st. Cont in pat to end of row. Turn.
2nd row: Work in pat to last 2 sts. Hdc2tog. Turn.
3rd row: Ch 2 (does not count as st). Hdc2tog. Cont in pat to end of row. Turn. Rep last 2 rows once more, then 2nd row once. 10 (11-11-12) sts. Fasten off.

Place markers for 4 buttons on Right Front in 2 rows (double breasted), spaced as follows:
Top row of 2 buttons positioned 2 rows down from

COZY HOODIE

neck edge—first button 1"/2.5cm from front edge; second button 4"/10cm from front edge (3"/7.5cm apart from each other). Bottom row of 2 buttons positioned 10 rows down from neck edge—first button 1"/2.5cm from front edge; second button 4"/10cm from front edge (3"/7.5cm apart from each other).

LEFT FRONT

Note: Work buttonhole row to correspond to markers on Right Front as follows:

Buttonhole row: (RS) (Work in pat to button marker. Ch 1. Skip next st) twice. Cont in pat to end of row.
Work from ** to ** as given for Right Front.

Shape Armhole

Next row: (RS) Sl st across first 3 sts. Ch 1. 1 sc in same sp as last sl st. Cont in pat to end of row. Turn. Cont even in pat over rem 29 (31-33-35) sts until armhole measures 6 rows less than Back (working buttonhole row to correspond to markers on Right Front), ending on a WS row.

Shape Neck

1st row: (RS) Work in pat across 14 (15-15-16) sts. Hdc2tog (neck edge). Turn. Leave rem sts unworked.
2nd row: Ch 2 (does not count as st). Hdc2tog. Cont in pat to end of row. Turn.
3rd row: Work in pat to last 2 sts. Hdc2tog. Turn.
4th row: As 2nd row.
5th row: Buttonhole row: (RS) (Work in pat to button marker. Ch 1. Skip next st) twice. Cont in pat to last 2 sts. Hdc2tog. Turn.
6th row: As 2nd row. 10 (11-11-12) sts. Fasten off.

SLEEVE (Make 2)

Ch 28 (30-30-34).
1st row: (RS) 1 sc in 2nd ch from hook. *1 dc in next ch. 1 sc in next ch. Rep from * to end of chain. Turn. 27 (29-29-33) sts.
Cont in pat as given for Back for 5 more rows.

Shape Sides

1st row: (RS-Inc row) Ch 3 (counts as dc). 1 sc in first dc. *1 dc in next sc. 1 sc in next dc. Rep from * to last 2 sts. 1 dc in next sc.(1 sc. 1 dc) in last dc. Turn.
2nd row: Ch 1. 1 sc in first dc. *1 dc in next sc. 1 sc in next dc. Rep from * to end of row. Turn.
3rd row: Ch 3 (counts as dc). *1 sc in next dc. 1 dc in next sc. Rep from* to end of row. Turn.
4th and 5th rows: As 2nd and 3rd rows.
Rep last 5 rows twice more. 33 (35-35-39) sts.
Cont even in pat until work from beg measures 7 (7½-8-8½)"/18 (19-20.5-21.5)cm, ending on a WS row.
Place markers at each end of last row.
Work 2 rows even in pat. Fasten off.

POCKETS

Ch 16 (16-18-18).
1st row: (RS) 1 sc in 2nd ch from hook. *1 dc in next ch. 1 sc in next ch. Rep from * to end of chain. Turn. 15 (15-17-17) sts.
Cont in pat as given for Back for 2 (2-2½-2½)"/5 (5-6.5-6.5)cm, ending on a WS row.

Shape Sides

1st row: (RS) Ch 2 (does not count as st). Hdc2tog. Cont in pat to last 2 sts. Hdc2tog. Turn.
Rep last row twice more. 9 (9-11-11) sts. Fasten off.

FINISHING

Sew shoulder seams. Sew in sleeves, placing rows above markers along unworked sts of Body to form square armholes. Sew side and sleeve seams, reversing seam for 1½"/4.5cm cuff turnback.

Hood

Place markers on neck edge 3"/7.5cm in from front edge. With RS facing, join yarn with sl st at Right Front neck marker. Ch 1. Work 71 (71-75-75) sc evenly around neck edge to opposite marker. Turn.
Next row: Ch 1. 1 sc in first sc. *1 dc in next sc. 1 sc in next sc. Rep from * end of row. Turn. Place marker on center back st.
Next row: (RS) Ch 3 (counts as dc). (1 sc in next dc. 1 dc in next sc) 17 (17-18-18) times. (1sc. 1 dc. 1 sc) all in next dc (center back st). (1 dc in next sc. 1 dc in next dc) 17 (17-18-18) times. 1 dc in last sc. Turn. Work 3 rows even in pat.
Next row: (RS) Ch 3 (counts as dc). (1 sc in next dc. 1 dc in next sc) 17 (17-18-18) times. 1 sc in next dc. (1 dc. 1 sc. 1 dc) all in next sc (center back st). (1 sc in next dc. 1 dc in next sc) 18 (18-19-19) times. Turn. Work 3 rows even in pat.
Next row: (RS) Ch 3 (counts as dc). (1 sc in next dc. 1 dc in next sc) 18 (18-19-19) times. (1 sc. 1 dc. 1 sc) all in next dc (center back st). (1 dc in next sc. 1 dc in next dc) 18 (18-19-19) times. 1 dc in last sc. Turn. 77 (77-81-81) sts.
Cont even in pat until Hood measures 8 (8½-8½-9)"/20.5

(21.5-21.5-23)cm from neck edge, ending on a WS row. Fasten off.
Fold Hood in half and sew top Hood seam.
Sew buttons and Pockets in position.

Pompom

Wind yarn around 3 fingers approx 100 times. Remove from fingers and tie tightly in center. Cut through each side of loops. Trim to a smooth round shape. Sew to end of Hood. •

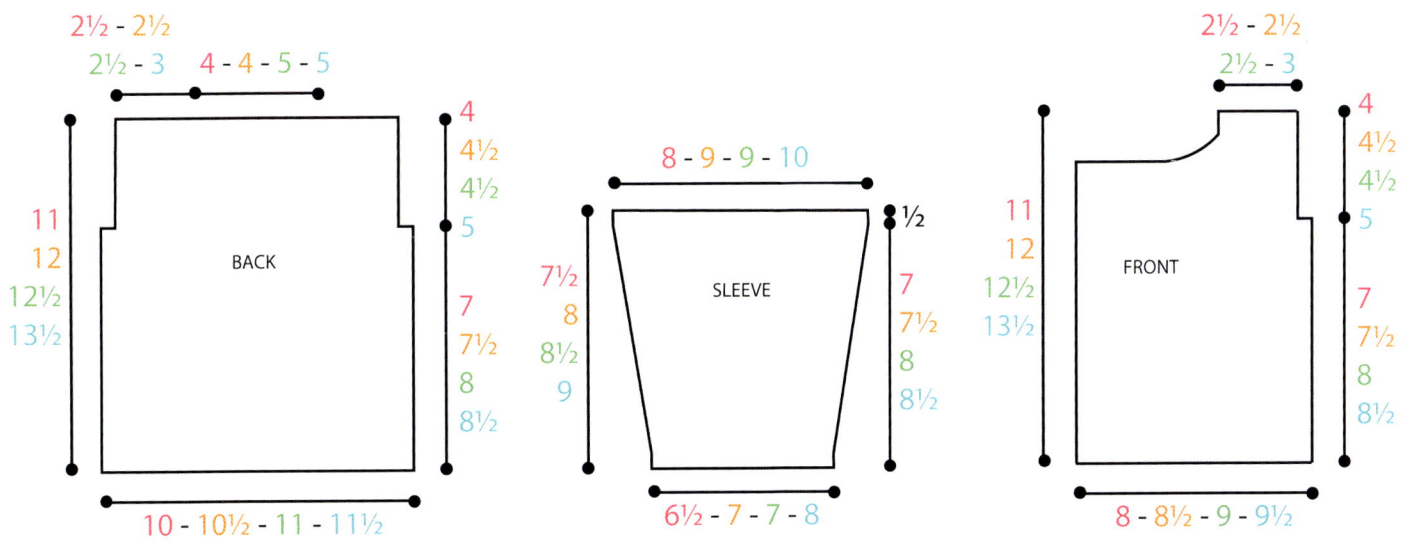

HAPPY BABY BLANKET

MEASUREMENTS

Basic Approx 40½"/105.5cm square

MATERIALS
Yarn

Bernat® *Baby Sport*™, 12.3oz/350g balls, each 1256yd/1148m (acrylic)
- 2 balls in #21230 Baby Green

Hook
- Size G/6 (4mm) crochet hook, *or size needed to obtain gauge*

GAUGE
16 dc and 8 rows = 4"/10cm using size G/6 (4mm) hook. *TAKE TIME TO CHECK GAUGE.*

BLANKET
Ch 160.

1st row: (RS) 1 dc in 4th ch from hook. 1 dc in each ch to end of chain. Turn. 158 dc.

2nd row: Ch 3 (counts as dc). 1 dc in next dc. *Ch 2. Skip next 2 dc. 1 dc in each of next 2 dc. Rep from * to end of row. Turn.

3rd row: Ch 3 (counts as dc). 1 dc in next dc. 2 dc in next ch-2 sp. *1 dc in each of next 2 dc. 2 dc in next ch-2 sp. Rep from * to last 2 dc. 1 dc in each of last 2 dc. Turn.

4th row: Ch 4 (counts at dc and ch 1). Skip next dc. 1 dc in each of next 2 dc. *Ch 2. Skip next 2 dc. 1 dc in each of next 2 dc. Rep from * to last 2 dc. Ch 1. Skip next dc. 1 dc in last dc. Turn.

5th row: Ch 3 (counts as dc). 1 dc in next ch-1 sp. 1 dc in each of next 2 dc. *2 dc in next ch-2 sp. 1 dc in each of next 2 dc. Rep from * to last 2 sts. 1 dc in 4th and 3rd ch of beg ch-4. Turn.

Rep 2nd to 5th rows for pat until Blanket measures approx 39"/99cm from beg, ending on a 3rd or 5th row of pat. Fasten off.

FINISHING
Edging

1st rnd: (RS) Join yarn with sl st to any corner of Blanket. Ch 1. Work 1 rnd of sc evenly around Blanket, having 3 sc in corners. Join with sl st to first sc.

2nd and 3rd rnds: Ch 1. 1 sc in each sc around, having 3 sc in corner sc. Join with sl st to first sc.•

CLOUDY DAY MOBILE

Easy

MEASUREMENTS
Approx 12"/30.5cm x 33"/84cm

MATERIALS
Yarn

Bernat® *Baby Blanket*™, 3½oz/100g balls, each approx 72yd/65m (polyester)
- 3 balls in #03008 Vanilla (A)
- 1 ball in #03734 Baby Teal (B)
- 1 ball in #03736 Seafoam (C)

Hook
- Size L/11 (8mm) crochet hook, *or size needed to obtain gauge*

Notions
- 12"/30cm embroidery hoop
- 1"/2.5cm split ring
- Stuffing

GAUGE
7 sc and 8 rows = 4"/10cm using size L/11 (8mm) hook. *TAKE TIME TO CHECK GAUGE.*

NOTES
- Ch 3 at beg of rnd counts as 1 dc.
- See diagrams on page 36.

MOBILE

Small Cloud (Make 4 pieces alike)
With A, ch 4. Join with sl st to first ch to form ring.
1st rnd: Ch 3. 11 dc in ring. Join with sl st to top of ch 3. 12 dc.
2nd rnd: (Sl st in next dc. 4 dc in next dc) 6 times. Sl st in first dc. Fasten off.

Medium Cloud (Make 4 pieces alike)
With A, ch 4. Join with sl st to first ch to form ring.
1st rnd: Ch 3. 11 dc in ring. Join with sl st to top of ch 3. 12 dc.
2nd rnd: Ch 3. 1 dc in same sp as last sl st. 2 dc in each dc around. Join with sl st to top of ch 3. 24 dc.
3rd rnd: (Sl st in next dc. Skip 1 dc. 5 dc in next dc. Skip 1 dc) 6 times. Sl st in first dc. Fasten off.

Large Cloud (Make 4 pieces alike)
With A, ch 4. Join with sl st to first ch to form ring.
1st rnd: Ch 3. 11 dc in ring. Join with sl st to top of ch 3. 12 dc.
2nd rnd: Ch 3. 1 dc in same sp as last sl st. 2 dc in each dc around. Join with sl st to top of ch 3. 24 dc.
3rd rnd: Ch 3. 1 dc in same sp as last sl st. 2 dc in each dc around. Join with sl st to top of ch 3. 48 dc.
4th rnd: (Sl st in next dc. Skip 2 dc. 5 dc in next dc. Skip 2 dc) 8 times. Sl st in first dc. Fasten off.

Joining Back and Front of Clouds
Place WS of 2 pieces tog. Join yarn with sl st to same sp as last sl st. Working through both thicknesses, ch 1. 1 sc in same sp as sl st. 1 sc in each sp around, stuffing lightly as you work. Join with sl st to first sc. Fasten off.

Hanging Loops
With A, make 6 chains, alternating lengths from 3"/7.5cm to 6"/15cm. Attach to top of Clouds as shown in photo.

Raindrops (Make 6 each with B and C)
Ch 4. Join with sl st to first ch to form ring.
1st rnd: Ch 1. (8 sc. Ch 1. 2 dc. Ch 1. 2 sc) all in ring. Join with sl st to first sc. Fasten off, leaving a 12"/30.5cm tail. Using tail, attach Raindrops to Clouds as pictured (3 on Large Clouds, 2 on Medium Clouds, and one on Small Clouds), alternating lengths from 3"/7.5cm to 8"/20.5cm.

CLOUDY DAY MOBILE

FINISHING

Using hanging loops, mount Clouds around embroidery hoop evenly. Make 3 crochet chains 24"/61cm long, and attach them around hoop evenly spaced. Join chains in center of hoop with split ring, as pictured.•

STITCH KEY

◯ = chain (ch)

• = slip stitch (sl st)

+ = single crochet (sc)

T = double crochet (dc)

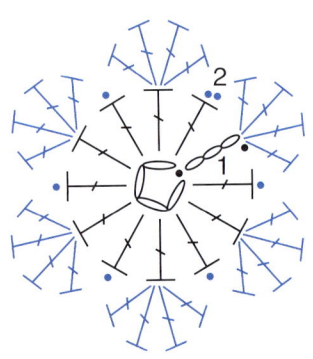

SMALL CLOUD

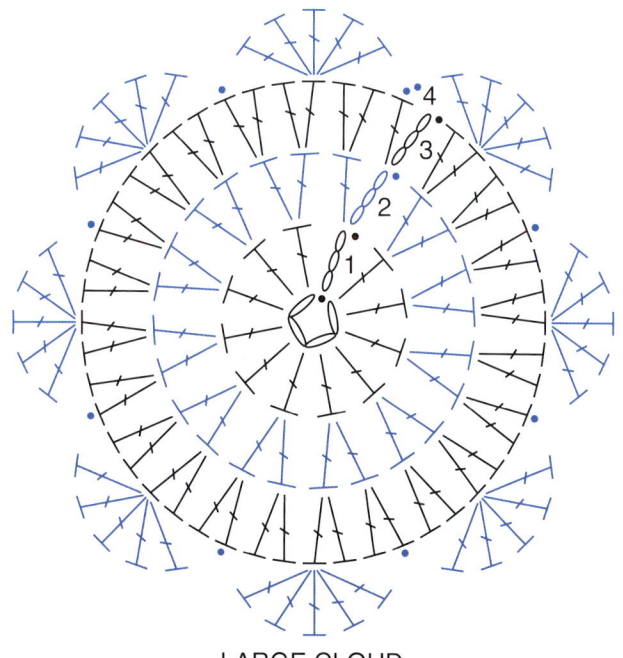

LARGE CLOUD

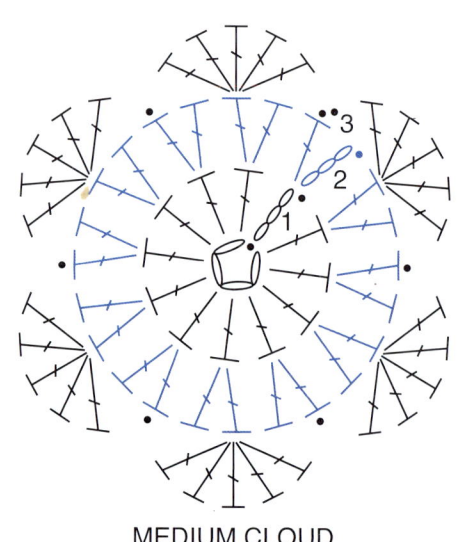

MEDIUM CLOUD

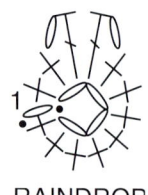

RAINDROP

CUFFED BOOTIES

Easy

SIZES
To fit infant 3 (6-12) months

MATERIALS
Yarn
Bernat® *Handicrafter*® *Cotton Solids*,
1¾oz/50g balls, each approx 80yd/73m (cotton)
• 1 (2-2) balls in #01002 Off White or #01746 Coral Rose or:

Bernat® *Handicrafter*® *Cotton Ombres*, 12oz/340g balls, each approx 573yd/524m (cotton)
• 1 (1-1) ball in #34029 Damask

Hook
• Size G/6 (4mm) crochet hook, *or size needed to obtain gauge*

GAUGE
14 sc and 15 rows = 4"/10cm using size G/6 (4mm) hook.
TAKE TIME TO CHECK GAUGE.

NOTE
• The instructions are written for smallest size. If changes are necessary for larger sizes the instructions will be written thus ( ).

BOOTIE (Make 2)
Cuff
Ch 16.
1st row: 1 sc in 2nd ch from hook. 1 sc in each ch to end of ch. Turn. 15 sc.
2nd row: Ch 1. Working in back loops only, 1 sc in each sc across. Rep last row until work from beg measures 6 (6¼-6½)"/15 (16-16.5)cm, ending with a RS row. Do not turn.

Foot
1st row: (RS). Ch 1. Work 23 (25-27) sc evenly along long edge of Cuff. Turn.
2nd row: Ch 1. 1 sc in each sc across. Fasten off.

Instep
1st row: With RS of work facing, skip first 7 (8-9) sc. Join yarn with sl st to next sc. Ch 1. 1 sc in same sp as last sl st. 1 sc in each of next 8 sc. Turn. Leave rem sts unworked. 9 sc.
2nd to 4th rows: Ch 1. 1 sc in each sc across. Turn.
5th row: Ch 1. Draw up a loop in each of next 2 sts. Yoh and draw through all 3 loops on hook—sc2tog made. 1 sc in each of next 5 sts. Sc2tog over next 2 sts. 7 sts. Fasten off. Sew back seam.

Foot
1st rnd: With RS of work facing, join yarn with sl st at center back. Ch 2 (counts as hdc). 1 hdc in each of next 6 (7-8) sts, 7 hdc down side of instep, 2 hdc in corner sc, 5 hdc across end of instep, 2 hdc in corner sc, 7 hdc along other side of instep, 1 hdc in each of next 7 (8-9) sts. Join with sl st in top of ch 2. 37 (39-41) hdc.
2nd rnd: Ch 2 (counts as hdc). *Yoh and draw up a loop around post of next st at back of work inserting hook from right to left. (Yoh and draw through 2 loops on hook) twice—1 dcbp made. Rep from * around. Join with sl st to top of ch 2.
3rd rnd: As 2nd rnd.
4th rnd: Ch 1. Sc2tog over first 2 sts. 1 sc in each of next 14 (15-16) sts. Sc2tog over next 2 sts. 1 sc in next st. Sc2tog over next 2 sts. 1 sc in each of next 14 (15-16) sts. Sc2tog over last 2 sts. Join with sl st to first st. 33 (35-37) sc.
5th rnd: Ch 1. Sc2tog over first 2 sts. 1 sc in each of next 12 (13-14) sc. Sc2tog over next 2 sts. 1 sc in next st. Sc2tog over next 2 sts. 1 sc in each of next 12 (13-14) sc. Sc2tog over last 2 sts. Join with sl st to first st. 29 (31-33) sts.
6th rnd: Ch 1. Sc2tog over first 2 sts. 1 sc in each of next 10 (11-12) sc. Sc2tog over next 2 sts. 1 sc in next st. Sc2tog over next 2 sts. 1 sc in each of next 10 (11-12) sc. Sc2tog over last 2 sts. Join with sl st to first st. 25 (27-29) sts.
7th rnd: Ch 1. Sc2tog over first 2 sts. 1 sc in each of next 8 (9-10) sc. Sc2tog over next 2 sts. 1 sc in next st. Sc2tog over next 2 sts. 1 sc in each of next 8 (9-10) sc. Sc2tog over last 2 sts. Join with sl st to first st. 21 (23-25) sts. Fasten off. Sew sole seam.•

QUICK & COZIEST BLANKET

Easy

MEASUREMENTS
Approx 40"/101.5cm square

MATERIALS
Yarn
Bernat® Softee® Chunky™, 3½oz/100g balls, each approx 108yd/99m (acrylic)
- 6 balls in #28418 Baby Pink (A)
- 2 balls in #28046 Gray Heather (B)

Hook
- Size L/11 (8mm) crochet hook, *or size needed to obtain gauge*

GAUGE
7 sc and 8 rows = 4"/10cm using size L/11 (8mm) hook.
TAKE TIME TO CHECK GAUGE.

STRIPE PATTERN
With A, work 6 rows.
With B, work 2 rows.
These 8 rows form Stripe Pat.

BLANKET
With A, ch 94.
1st row: (RS) 2 dc in 4th ch from hook (counts as 3 dc). *1 dc in each of next 5 ch. Ch 3. Skip next 3 ch. 1 sc in next ch. Ch 3. Skip next 3 ch. 1 dc in each of next 5 ch.** (2 dc. Ch 1. 2 dc) in next ch. Rep from * 3 times more, then from * to ** once. 3 dc in last ch. Turn.
2nd row: Ch 1. 1 sc in first dc. 1 sc in each of next 7 dc*. Ch 2. (1 dc. Ch 1. 1 dc) in next sc. Ch 2. 1 sc in each of next 7dc.** Ch 1. 1 sc in each of next 7 dc. Rep from * 3 times more, then from * to ** once. 1 sc in top of turning ch. Turn.
3rd row: Ch 3. 2 dc in first sc.* 1 dc in each of next 5 sc. Ch 3. Skip next 2 sc. 1 sc in next ch-1 sp. Ch 3. Skip next 2 sc. 1 dc in each of next 5 sc.** (2 dc. Ch 1. 2 dc) in next ch-1 sp. Rep from * 3 times more, then from * to ** once. 3 dc in last sc. Turn.
Last 2 rows form pat, first 3 rows of Stripe Pat are completed.
Cont in Stripe Pat until Blanket from beg measures approx 39"/99cm, ending with 6 rows of A.

FINISHING
Side Edging
On RS, join A with sl st to bottom right corner. Ch 1. Work 1 row of sc evenly along side edge. Fasten off. Rep for other side.•

SUNSHINE PILLOW

Easy

MEASUREMENTS
Approx 15"/38cm diameter, including Sun Rays

MATERIALS
Yarn (6)
Bernat® *Baby Blanket*™, 3½oz/100g balls, each approx 72yd/65m (polyester)
• 2 balls in #03615 Baby Yellow

Yarn (4)
Bernat® *Super Value*™, 7oz/197g balls, each approx 426yd/389m (acrylic)
• 10yd/9m in #07421 Black for embroidery

Hook
• Size L/11 (8mm) crochet hook, *or size needed to obtain gauge*

Notion
• Stuffing

GAUGE
7 sc and 8 rows = 4"/10cm using size L/11 (8mm) hook.
TAKE TIME TO CHECK GAUGE.

FRONT AND BACK (Make Alike)
Ch 2.
1st rnd: 8 sc in 2nd ch from hook. Join with sl st to first sc.
2nd rnd: Ch 1. 2 sc in each sc around. Join with sl st to first sc. 16 sc.
3rd rnd: Ch 1. 1 sc in first sc. 2 sc in next sc. *1 sc in next sc. 2 sc in next sc. Rep from * around. Join with sl st to first sc. 24 sc.
4th rnd: Ch 1. 1 sc in each of first 2 sc. 2 sc in next sc. *1 sc in each of next 2 sc. 2 sc in next sc. Rep from * around. Join with sl st to first sc. 32 sc.
5th rnd: Ch 1. 1 sc in each of first 3 sc. 2 sc in next sc. *1 sc in each of next 3 sc. 2 sc in next sc. Rep from * around. Join with sl st to first sc. 40 sc.
6th to 9th rnds: Cont in same manner, inc 8 sts evenly spaced on every rnd to 72 sc. Fasten off.

Seaming
With WS of Front and Back facing each other join yarn with sl st through both thicknesses to any sc. Ch 1. Working through both thicknesses, sc in each sc around leaving a small opening for stuffing. Stuff Pillow. Complete rnd of sc to close opening. Join with sl st to first sc. Do not fasten off. Cont as follows for Sun Rays:

First Sun Ray
1st row: Ch 1. 1 sc in each of first 6 sc. Turn. Leave rem sts unworked. 6 sc.
**2nd row: Ch 1. Skip first sc. 1 sc in each of next 3 sc. Sc2tog. Turn. 4 sc.
3rd row: Ch 1. Skip first sc. 1 sc in next sc. Sc2tog. Turn. 2 sc.
4th row: Ch 1. Sc2tog. Fasten off.**

Second to Twelfth Sun Rays
With RS facing, join yarn with sl st to next skipped sc of joining rnd. Ch 1. 1 sc in same sp as last sl st. 1 sc in each of next 5 sc. Turn. Leave rem sts unworked. 6 sc. Work from ** to ** as given for First Sun Ray.

FINISHING
With black yarn, embroider Eyes and Mouth using chain stitch as seen in photo.•

CHAIN STITCH

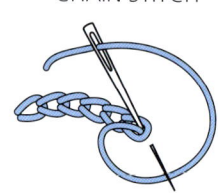

BIB & BOOTIES SET

Easy

MEASUREMENTS
To fit size 6–12 months.

MATERIALS
Yarn

Bernat® Handicrafter® Cotton, 1¾oz/50g balls, each approx 80yd/73m (cotton)
- 2 balls in #01001 White (A)
- 2 balls in #01111 Mod Blue (B)

Hook
- Size G/6 (4mm) crochet hook, *or size needed to obtain gauge*

Notion
- Button

GAUGE
14 hdc and 10 rows = 4"/10cm using size G/6 (4mm) hook. *TAKE TIME TO CHECK GAUGE.*

BIB
With A, ch 21.

1st row: (RS) 1 hdc in 3rd ch from hook. 1 hdc in each of next 2 ch. *Ch 1. Skip next ch. 1 hdc in each of next 3 ch. Rep from * to end of ch. Turn. 19 sts.

2nd row: Ch 2. 2 hdc in first st. 1 hdc in each st or ch-1 sp to last st. 2 hdc in last st. Join B. Turn.

3rd row: Ch 1. 1 sc in each of first 4 sts. *(Yoh) twice and draw up a loop in skipped ch of foundation ch 2 rows below in front of work. (Yoh and draw through 2 loops on hook) 3 times—long tr made. Skip next st (behind long tr). 1 sc in each of next 3 sts. Rep from * to last st. 1 sc in last st. Turn.

4th row: Ch 1. 2 sc in first st. 1 sc in each st to last st. 2 sc in last st. Join A. Turn.

5th row: Ch 2. 1 hdc in first st. *Ch 1. Skip next st. 1 hdc in each of next 3 sts. Rep from * to last 2 sts. Ch 1. Skip next st. 1 hdc in last st. Ch 2. Turn.

6th row: 2 hdc in first st. 1 hdc in each st or ch sp to last st. 2 hdc in last st. Join B. Turn.

7th row: Ch 1. 1 sc in each of first 2 sts. *Long tr in next skipped st 2 rows below. Skip next st (behind long tr). 1 sc in each of next 3 sts. Rep from * to last 3 sts. Long tr in next skipped st 2 rows below. Skip next st (behind long tr). 1 sc in each of next 2 sts. Turn.

8th row: Ch 1. 2 sc in first st. 1 sc in each st to last st. 2 sc in last st. Join A. Turn. 27 sts. Cont even in pat as placed in last 8 rows for 12 more rows.

Shape neck

1st row: (RS) With A, ch 2. Pat across 6 sts. Yoh and draw up a loop in next st. Draw up a loop in next st. Yoh and draw through all loops on hook—hdc2tog made. Turn. Leave rem sts unworked.

2nd row: Ch 2. Hdc2tog over first 2 sts. Pat to end of row. Join B. Ch 1. Turn.

3rd row: Ch 2. Pat to last 2 sts. Draw up a loop in each of next 2 sts. Yoh and draw through 3 loops on hook—sc2tog made. Turn. 5 sts. Work 6 rows even in pat.

Next row: (WS) Ch 2. 2 hdc in first st. Pat to last 2 sts. Hdc2tog. Join B. Turn.

Next row: Ch 1. Sc2tog. Pat to last st. 2 sc in last st. Turn.

Next row: Ch 1. 2 sc in first st. Pat to last 2 sts. Sc2tog. Join A. Turn.

Next row: Ch 2. Hdc2tog. Pat to last st. 2 hdc in last st. Turn.

Next row: Ch 2. 2 hdc in first st. Pat to last 2 sts. Hdc2tog. Fasten off. With RS of work facing, skip next 11 sts. Join A with sl st to next st. Ch 2. Hdc2tog over this st and next st. Pat to end of row. Turn. Work to correspond to first side, reversing all shapings.

FINISHING
Edging

Join B with sl st to top left corner of neck edge. Ch 1. 1 sc in same sp as last sl st. Work 1 row sc evenly around all edges. Join with sl st to first sc.

Next rnd: Working around outer edge only, ch 1.

Working from left to right, instead of from right to left as usual, work 1 reverse sc in each sc to opposite side. Fasten off. With B, make button loop at center back on left side. Sew button in position.

BOOTIE (Make 2)

With B, ch 28.

1st row: (RS) 1 sc in 2nd ch from hook. 1 sc in each ch to end of ch. 27 sts. Turn.

2nd row: Ch 1. 1 sc in each sc to end of row. Join A. Turn.

3rd row: With A, ch 2. 1 hdc in first st. *Ch 1. Skip next st. 1 hdc in each of next 3 sts. Rep from * to last 2 sts. Ch 1. Skip next st. 1 hdc in next st. Turn.

4th row: Ch 2. 1 hdc in first st. 1 hdc in each st or ch-1 sp to end of row. Join B. Turn.

BIB & BOOTIES SET

5th row: With B, ch 1. 1 sc in first st. *Long tr in next skipped ch 2 rows below. Skip next st (behind long tr). 1 sc in each of next 3 sts. Rep from * to last 2 sts. Long tr in next skipped ch 2 rows below. Skip next st (behind long tr). 1 sc in last st. Turn.
6th row: Ch 1. 1 sc in each of first 4 sts. *Sc2tog. 1 sc in each of next 4 sts. Rep from * to last 3 sts. 1 sc in each of last 3 sts. Turn. 23 sts.
7th row: (Eyelet row) Ch 1. 1 sc in each of first 2 sts. *Ch 1. Skip next st. 1 sc in each of next 2 sts. Rep from * to last 2 sts. 1 sc in each of last 2 sts. Turn.
8th row: Ch 1. 1 sc in each st or ch 1 sp to end of row. Fasten off.

Instep
1st row: With RS of work facing, skip first 7 sts. Join B with sl st to next st. Ch 1. 1 sc in same sp. 1 sc in each of next 8 sts. Turn. 9 sts.
2nd row: Ch 2. 1 hdc in each st to end of row. Turn.
3rd row: Ch 1. 1 sc in each st to end of row. Turn.
4th row: As 2nd row.
5th row: Ch 1. Sc2tog. 1 sc in each st to last 2 sts. Sc2tog. Fasten off. Sew center back seam. With RS of work facing, join B with sl st at center back seam. Ch 1. 1 sc in each of next 7 sts. Work 5 sc down side of instep. 3 sc in corner sc. 5 sc across end of instep. 3 sc in corner sc. Work 5 sc along other side of instep. 1 sc in each of next 7 sts. Join with sl st to first st. 35 sts.
Next rnd: Ch 1. 1 sc in each st around. Join A with sl st to first st.
Next rnd: With A, ch 1. Working in back loops only work 1 sc in each st around. Join with sl st to first st.
Next rnd: Ch 1. Sc2tog. 1 sc in each of next 13 sts. Sc2tog. 1 sc in next st. Sc2tog. 1 sc in each of next 13 sts. Sc2tog. Join with sl st to first st.
Next rnd: Ch 1. Sc2tog. 1 sc in each of next 11 sts. Sc2tog. 1 sc in next st. Sc2tog. 1 sc in each of next 11 sts. Sc2tog. Join with sl st to first st.
Next rnd: Ch 1. Sc2tog. 1 sc in each of next 9 sts. Sc2tog. 1 sc in next st. Sc2tog. 1 sc in each of next 9 sts. Sc2tog. Join with sl st to first st. Fasten off. Join center foot seam.

FINISHING
Drawstring
With A, chain a length to measure 16"/40.5cm. Fasten off. Weave drawstring through eyelet row. Knot ends of drawstring.•